HENRY SIDGWICK
SCIENCE AND FAITH
IN VICTORIAN ENGLAND

UNIVERSITY OF
NEWCASTLE UPON TYNE
PUBLICATIONS

HENRY SIDGWICK
SCIENCE AND FAITH
IN VICTORIAN ENGLAND

———

The Riddell Memorial Lectures
Thirty-ninth Series

BY

D. G. JAMES
Formerly Vice-Chancellor of the
University of Southampton

———

WITH

A MEMOIR OF THE AUTHOR

BY GWYN JONES

LONDON
OXFORD UNIVERSITY PRESS
NEW YORK TORONTO
1970

Oxford University Press, Ely House, London W. 1

GLASGOW NEW YORK TORONTO MELBOURNE WELLINGTON
CAPE TOWN SALISBURY IBADAN NAIROBI DAR ES SALAAM LUSAKA ADDIS ABABA
BOMBAY CALCUTTA MADRAS KARACHI LAHORE DACCA
KUALA LUMPUR SINGAPORE HONG KONG TOKYO

SBN 19 713910 8

PRINTED IN GREAT BRITAIN
AT THE UNIVERSITY PRESS, OXFORD
BY VIVIAN RIDLER
PRINTER TO THE UNIVERSITY

CONTENTS

INTRODUCTION

THE calamity of the death of Gwilym James in December 1968, while he was preparing the lectures which he intended to deliver in the spring of 1969, has caused this to be the first volume in the series to contain Riddell Lectures that were not delivered to an audience in the University in Newcastle upon Tyne. Those of us who had been concerned in the invitation to Gwilym James learned with sad relief that he had gone so far in the composition of the three lectures that, with careful editing, they could be put into shape for publication. This task was undertaken by his widow Mrs. Gwynneth James, assisted by Mrs. Rhiannon Aaron who typed the manuscript, to both of whom the University is deeply grateful for their painstaking care. Even so, the text must be regarded as an incomplete draft, and not the finished version that Gwilym James would have sent to the press if he had been spared to deliver the lectures and thereafter to revise the text.

But the lectures are in a sufficiently finished state to be enjoyed by the audience which had been eager to hear them in April 1969, and by the wider public which purchases the Riddell Lectures as they are published year by year.

This volume is a worthy addition to the series. The theme is one of deep significance, and Henry Sidgwick is a fascinating character. Gwilym James had prepared himself, by his study of Wordsworth, Tennyson, Matthew Arnold, and other writers and thinkers of the Victorian Age, to interpret the strains that racked

Henry Sidgwick and to assess his influence upon his contemporaries and his pupils.

Many people think that the lectures were established in memory of Sir Walter Buchanan Riddell, the 12th Baronet, Principal of Hertford College, Oxford, from 1922 to 1930, and Chairman of the University Grants Committee from 1930 until his untimely death in 1934. But the first Riddell Lectures were delivered in 1928, which happened to be 400 years after Charles I had created a Riddell ancestor to be a Baronet of Nova Scotia. It was as a memorial to Sir Walter Riddell's father, Sir John Walter Buchanan Riddell, that the lectures were endowed by an anonymous donor whom we now know to have been Mr. Wilfred Hall, a close friend and neighbour to the Riddells at Hepple in Northumberland. The terms of his gift provided that 'the subject matter of the lectures is to be the relation between religion and contemporary development of thought, particularly in the spheres of Natural Science, Archaeology, Psychology or Philosophy, with particular emphasis on and reference to the bearing of such developments on the ethics and tenets of Christianity'. If the Riddell Lectures had been established in his lifetime Henry Sidgwick would have been a natural choice as lecturer. Now through this penetrating study by Gwilym James we can assess the contribution of Henry Sidgwick to the evolution of new attitudes to 'the ethics and tenets of Christianity'.

In the Memoir which follows, Professor Gwyn Jones, C.B.E., of the University of Wales, one of Gwilym James's oldest friends, writes of him in a more personal way.

C. I. C. BOSANQUET

December 1969

GWILYM JAMES

A MEMOIR

I FIRST met Gwilym James on the day he was appointed to the teaching staff here at Cardiff. That was in 1937, and it seems a very short time ago. I held out my hand and said 'Maes-yr-Haf': he took it and said 'Richard Savage'. All men know by what they may first be greeted, and none by what they shall, if at all, be remembered.

He was on instant recognition a high-flyer, alert, deft, generous, sensitive, of quick sympathy, well read, and intelligent. Even had he not become so dear a friend I would think him one of the most engaging men I have met. He had some good friends in College already, B. J. Morse, poet, translator, cosmopolitan, and polyglot, and David Williams the historian of modern Wales. The first of these he had known at Aberystwyth, where his term coincided with that of various distinguished and eccentric survivors of the First World War; with the second he had a West Wales affiliation, for though he was born and schooled at Pontypool in the ancient kingdom of Gwent, he lived long spells with camphored aunts in Pwyll's seven commotes of Dyfed. I wish I had listened with a more riveting care to the largely incidental reminiscence of his early years, but who at thirty thinks on death and elegies?

It was at Aber that he met his wife Dilys. She was of the wide race of Joneses, but her father, headmaster of the famed seminary of brains and rugby football at

Neath, sought to alleviate our Welsh penury of sur-
names by having her christened Dilys Cledwyn. To
brief avail. At Cardiff they came to live in Rhiwbina,
across the road from my wife Alice and me. We were
short of money but rich in human possessions; with the
Great Depression behind us unreservedly happy; with
the Second World War ahead unremittingly optimistic.
The Gwilyms had two children, and were soon to have
two more. It was a pleasure to ask 'How's Dilys today?'
merely to hear the Shakespearian rejoinder, 'She
rounds apace, she rounds apace!' I owned an aged
Lanchester, as sumptuous as she was slothful, and it
was understood that I would be keeping her fly-wheel
unctuously fluid against the great day. And so it happened
that in the fullness of time it was Alice and I who
delivered the Gwilyms to the nursing home and later
back to Rhiwbina with their tiny twins. If this sounds
less than solemn, we all loved each other dearly, and
there was nothing to be solemn about.

I recall that after leaving Aber Gwilym went up to
Cambridge, where by his own testimony he read deeply
and had resolution enough not to take a degree. That
he then went in for extra-mural teaching is not sur-
prising. He was not only raised in but was part of the
South Wales radical-nonconformist tradition, and had
been powerfully influenced by the local extra-mural
silver-tongued Fabian spell-binder while yet a schoolboy
in Pontypool. He had a strong sense of social service,
and though he grew more sceptical of the heaven-
sent nature of thunder on the right and lightning on
the left, stayed a political and religious animal to the
end of his life. The University was the right place for
him, if only because its demands stretched his mind,

and gave him both peers and an audience; but while at Cardiff he undertook evening classes in far-off Ebbw Vale, partly from a sense of service, partly, and naturally, because his infant family needed the money. At Cardiff, too, he taught the Cooks, nubile pursuers of the Domestic Arts, and found them as hard to teach as they were easy to look at.

But more than anything else he was a scholar and critic, and somehow or other he kept writing. He was well grounded in philosophy as in literature, and there could have been no better Chair for him than that at Bristol, which he occupied with high distinction after his five years at Cardiff and a couple in the Ministry of Whatever.

He was a good teacher and fought down a high-strung nervousness to become an admirable and attractive lecturer. He was at all times a stimulating disputant, keen, thrusting, courteous, and merciful. He became a master of the after-dinner speech and its analogues, and his elegant addresses of welcome on formal occasions were a delight to all who received their benediction. He was a prime mover in establishing in 1947 the annual conference of Professors of English in Great Britain, from which grew the International Conference of Professors of English, and did more than anyone by personal example to make them warm and friendly assemblies, without side or stuffiness. Everyone thawed in his presence; his charm was not extruded, it was part of his being; his kindness was not indiscriminate, but by inclination it was constant.

I know very little about his years as Vice-Chancellor at Southampton. We visited there, and the Gwilyms visited us at Aberystwyth; we were together on many occasions, and his quick affection had neither slowed nor blunted. Whether he should have become a Vice-Chancellor I don't know. It never looked the job for me, and I should have thought it was still less the job for him. But I have many times heard him say that it was no good academics grousing about unacademic V-Cs if they weren't prepared to do the job themselves. I don't doubt his conscience had a sharper cutting edge than mine—and he had four children to provide for and educate. Still, in the line of duty every Vice-Chancellor has to sweep the legs from under you from time to time, and how Gwilym James hardened himself to this imperative exercise I don't know. Obviously he was highly successful at Southampton during a time of change and expansion. My assumption was that he would enjoy the office for five years, endure it for a further three, and then seek the comparative haven of a Chair of English. In fact he both enjoyed and endured it longer, so that he came to suffer acutely from his inability to find time for sustained bouts of writing. He was full of plans for books, enough to occupy ten years of undisturbed literary composition. He saw this as both pleasure and vocation. 'It's no good,' he would say about the drearier acreages of academic writing. 'These chaps are dead. Their stuff is dead. It's got to be alive, alive!' As he was himself, in everything he did, said, and wrote, intensely alive.

In the event he did disentangle himself from the coils and toils of university administration. He and Dilys had for some years been discussing where and how they would live. He had received several invitations to teach, more or less on his own terms, and in particular they were pledged to go for a while to Yale. It was now they bought a cottage in the picturesque Suffolk village of Lavenham, so that they would have a home to return to from America. Physically Gwilym was not in the best of shape, and Dilys was feeling the strains and stresses of a busy and out-giving life. To a claustro-phobic Welsh eye like mine the American visit looked a mistake, and retirement to Lavenham a disaster. As it happened, this last was most cruelly forestalled. As they were settling into their new home in August 1965 Dilys suffered a severe stroke, from which she died, still unconscious, a few hours later.

Theirs had been a close, loving, and sufficient rela-tionship, and her death was a disabling blow from which he took a long time to recover, even partially. Without the support of his children his state would have been still worse. After a good deal of thought he took up his visiting professorship at Yale, where I stayed with him briefly the following March. He was surrounded by kindness, prized by his students, and on the best of terms with colleagues, college servants, everybody. But deeply riven, and his thoughts were back on Wales. We had not been alone for twenty minutes when his face broke and he said, 'I want to tell you about Dilys. I want you to tell Alice.' He stood up, I stood up, we embraced and we cried. Then he talked, and I talked, he achieved a new peacefulness, and we fortified our Welsh occasion with Scotland's dearest and Ken-tucky's best. Music had come to play a big part in his life: for five days our corner of Timothy Dwight College reverberated to Bach and Purcell; even at 6.30 in the morning, which seemed excessive to a boy nurtured on Handel and the Three Valleys' Festival. He appeared to be (I can't avoid the word) transported by these ocean-swells of sound; he would conduct, gesture, pirouette, then catch my eye, laugh, and say (and he never said a truer word): 'But you want your breakfast!'

I wondered whether music was taking the place of poetry for him—an almost unthinkable thought. Certainly it was bound up with his religious feelings. His belief in another life was absolute. 'We must believe in another life. Or this one would be unendurable.' And, 'There has to be a meaning. We are more than brutes, or we are nothing.' In his mouth these sentences were not platitudes: they vibrated with a passionate conviction. He had borrowed or bought a substantial library, was writing to a schedule, and talked about three big and three small books he hoped to see emerge as a coherent scheme of study dealing with literature, philosophy, religion, and society in the centuries he knew best. More immediately he was checking the typescript of *The Dream of Prospero*, which was to appear from the Clarendon Press the following year. Probably it is association which makes this for me the most delightful though not the most important of his books.

At the end of the College year he returned to wherever was to be home. Lavenham was impossible, and he removed to Aberystwyth, whose College and people had always been close to his heart. It was here that he met a lifelong friend of his and his wife's, Gwynneth Chegwidden, and married again. They bought a house near the College playing-fields, with a view of the ancient hill-fortresses on Pen Dinas. They made extensive alterations, and paid due attention to the library and study. We all rejoiced for him. They came to visit us, and he was on top of his form, eager, gay, assured, a great giver and taker of human affection. We arranged to meet in the summer at Dublin, at the International Conference of Professors of English. Here too, in Valley phrase, he was in his oils, but from time to time very tired. I don't think it was in his nature to live at half-pressure. We saw them again in November 1968, when they came to Cardiff on a family mission. He was dressed against the cold in an impressive down-to-the-knees tweed overcoat and a capacious down-to-the-ears tweed cap, and with his bright eyes, keen features, mobile expression, questing air, and robin-like quickness of manner looked a literary Sherlock Holmes. We had a noble day and talked our heads off, about the future more than the past, of change in the universities, books to be written, things to be done. And, of course, people. I thought then, and recall now, that in more than thirty years' talk, together or in company, I never heard him say an ill-natured thing. Critical, yes; tart, yes; caustic, yes; but ill-natured, grudging, cruel, no. We settled on a visit to Aber in the spring, waved our fourfold goodbyes, and never saw him again. In early December we were startled and grieved to hear of his sudden death.

There is a lot left for others to say about this gifted and delightful man. His excellence as professor, vice-chancellor, teacher, and literary critic will be recorded by a more informed hand. He was an exciting talker, and I always hear his voice in his books, which have given me insights into literature and the human spirit informing it that I should otherwise not have had. He was neither censor nor preacher: he just assumed that you were working, reading, writing, thinking, doing, as he was himself. He raised the spirits and

quality of any gathering of which he was part; he was
the living justification of the idea of a University, and
in every way a choice human being. He was the good
citizen, at a high level of thought and feeling, and not
only those near to him but the institutions he served,
both civic and educational, stand barer at his going.

GWYN JONES

December 1969

I

RUGBY AND CAMBRIDGE

HENRY SIDGWICK was born on 31 May 1838 at Skipton in the West Riding of Yorkshire. He was to be, in many ways, a typical as well as a highly individual Victorian: of some of these ways I shall have something to say. But I remark now that he was born the year after Queen Victoria came to the throne, and died a year or so before her. His life fairly spanned her reign: he qualifies, in terms of years merely, and pretty accurately, to be called a Victorian.

His father, William Sidgwick, had been to Trinity College, Cambridge, in the twenties and had taken Orders. But he died young, in 1841, leaving his widow with five children. Mrs. Sidgwick was, happily, not threatened by poverty; and she and her young family moved about a good deal, in Wales and in England, in a vain attempt to save the health of one of the little girls. Henry thus had a disturbed infancy: he was an excitable child and acquired a certain stammer which he was never to lose and which was later, it was said, to add to the charm of his conversation. But at length, in 1852, he went to Rugby School.

The circumstances of his going to Rugby are of great interest. William Sidgwick had always severely criticized the public schools. But he died a year before Thomas Arnold and had not known of Arnold's success at Rugby. It was Edward White Benson, later Archbishop of Canterbury, a cousin of William Sidgwick but only nine years older than Henry, who persuaded Mrs. Sidgwick to send Henry to Rugby. Benson, a Trinity man, took the Tripos in 1852, and, in the course of that summer, was offered a Mastership at Rugby. He had read Stanley's *Life of Arnold* when only a boy; Arnold became one of his heroes; and he gladly took the chance of teaching the Rugby Sixth form in Arnold's Library. Thus it came about that both Benson and Sidgwick went together to Rugby in the September of 1852. In the summer of 1853 Mrs. Sidgwick moved house again, and settled in Rugby in a pleasant roomy house on the edge of the town.

Henry Sidgwick lived at home for two years after his mother had come to Rugby; and soon Edward Benson left his lodgings to join the Sidgwick household. Benson had frequently visited the Sidgwick family in their various places of residence; and now, in Rugby, he joined them. It was a remarkable household. There were the four Sidgwick children: William, soon to become a Scholar of Corpus, Oxford; Henry and Arthur at Rugby School and both full of promise; and Mary, the youngest, who was twelve years old when her husband-to-be, Edward Benson, came to live under the Sidgwick roof. Benson, naturally masterful, was virtually head of the household. Mrs. Sidgwick was unfailingly gentle and affectionate. It seems to have been an extraordinarily happy family.

II

When we consider the course which Henry Sidgwick's life was to take, the role which Benson played in it in these early years must hold our attention.

Benson was born in 1829, in Birmingham, and had gone to King Edward's School there. Prince Lee was headmaster; and—it seems incredible—Westcott and Lightfoot were both pupils of the school: Westcott was senior boy when Benson went there and Lightfoot a year older than Benson. Westcott he did not come to know; but with Lightfoot, like himself a day-boy, he quickly became friends; both were deeply religious; and this was to be the dearest and the longest friendship of Benson's life.

Benson went to Trinity in 1848 and thereby made it still more likely that Sidgwick would go there too. Lightfoot had gone to Cambridge the year before, and there was a voluminous correspondence between them during this year of separation. I refer to only one letter in this correspondence, written by Benson, who had heard Newman preach in Birmingham and now described him and his manner of preaching. I cannot now quote from this letter: but it shows clearly enough the mixture of alarm and fascination which Newman aroused in Benson's mind. And Henry Sidgwick was to write, after Benson's death, that he had formed the impression that Benson had, while an undergraduate, undergone great struggle and anxiety on account of the attraction he felt towards the Church of Rome.

Sidgwick had been brought up in a pious household; and here now was Benson exercising a profound influence over his mind. 'Through Benson's talk in home life,

his readings . . . his advice and stimulus . . . his intellectual influence over me was completely maintained',
Sidgwick was to write. Nor was Benson's rule over
Sidgwick's mind maintained at all by fear. 'When I
did what he advised, it was not from awe of him and
fear of blame, but from a conviction that he was right
and a desire to be like him.' In the same reminiscences
of the Archbishop which he wrote for A. C. Benson's
Life of his father, Sidgwick explains that Benson was
shy of using edifying and religious talk in the course of
teaching; then, after recalling a lesson given by Benson
on Tacitus, he says,

he did occasionally let the deeply religious view of the world
and life that was habitual to him flash out impressively.
At the end of the lesson I refer to, after making us feel the
gloomy indignation of Tacitus at the corruption of his
times, he, closing the book, reminded us how the Founder
of the religion which was destined to purify the over-
civilized world was at this very time on earth. It was only
a couple of sentences, but I remember going away startled
into a reverent appreciation of the providential scheme of
human history which was not soon to be forgotten.

Here no doubt was the deepest thing in Benson; and
because at Rugby and for the early part of his undergraduate time at Cambridge, Benson's influence over him
was far stronger than that of anyone else, we may suppose that it was at this time the deepest thing in Sidgwick. 'Not soon to be forgotten', says Sidgwick; it was
no doubt to decline in brightness in Sidgwick's mind;
but it was by no means, as we shall see, to be obliterated,
or the sense of it destroyed.

III

Sidgwick made fast progress at Rugby. By the end of his first year in the Sixth, when he was just past seventeen, he had proved better than his seniors and had taken the first Exhibition at Trinity. But more remarkable than the speed of his progress was the range and breadth of his studies and interests: he was as proficient in Mathematics as in Classics, and read widely in poetry as well as in prose. Of poetry he had powers of intense enjoyment, and a prodigious memory for it which he never lost: throughout his life he astonished and delighted his friends by his power of declaiming poetry which had moved him: his memory for it seems to have been almost effortless. Already then we see him, in his school days, possessing strong analytical powers of mind along with equal gifts for poetical appreciation. Neither of these powers was he ever to lose. The author of *The Methods of Ethics* will not overcome the poet in him.

In October 1855 Sidgwick went to Cambridge, which was to be his home until his death in 1900. As an undergraduate he collected bundles of prizes, took the mathematical and classical Triposes in 1859, and went on to take the Chancellor's Medal. In October of that year he was elected a Fellow of Trinity and appointed to an Assistant Tutorship in Classics. He thus promptly and early began his life's work as a teacher and writer. 1859, then, was a critical year in his life. In that year also his sister Mary married Edward Benson.

His academic successes were incidental to the rapid growth of his mind. In 1859 he was only twenty-one years old; but as early as 1857, in his second year at

Cambridge, his mind and sensibility were changing. He said that for the first half of his undergraduate time Benson's influence over him was complete; 'I had', he said, 'no other ideal except to be a scholar as like him as possible.' But, by the end of his undergraduate days, deep and permanent differences had grown up between them; by this time they seemed to inhabit different worlds. In 1859, when he took his degree and Fellowship and Benson became his brother-in-law, the old intimacy was at an end: at least, 'in spite of an intimacy never clouded by any consciousness of change in our relation of personal affection—my reminiscences of his talk and judgements as to his views in later years are rather those of an outsider, intellectually speaking'. So Sidgwick wrote, many years later, after Benson's death: they became outsiders to each other; it may be said of them that they came to shake hands as over a vast gulf, and to embrace from the ends of opposed winds.

The new master, whose influence was now to over-come Sidgwick's discipleship to Benson, was John Stuart Mill. But before Mill's influence came to work strongly upon him, there had been, for a decisive event in his life, his election in the Michaelmas Term of his second year to the remarkable Cambridge society called the Apostles. It was this society which prepared him to take the impact of Mill's doctrines in his later undergraduate years. It was through the channel of the Apostles that the great stream of liberalism, as Newman called it, poured into Sidgwick's mind; and it helped to make submission to Mill's doctrines, then at the height of their influence, easy and natural. The society of the Apostles had come into existence in 1820, led by John Sterling and F. D. Maurice; it had had, and had still, a profound liberalizing influence. In the same decade, before Maurice left Cambridge, Newman had begun, in St. Mary's at Oxford, his University sermons, and the opposing power was beginning to gather strength. 'I thought', Newman was to write in the *Apologia*, 'that if Liberalism once got a footing within the Church of England, it was sure of victory in the end.' Sidgwick took service now with liberalism and science and 'reason'; he was indeed to lose heart at times and think of Newman; but it was John Stuart Mill now who more than anyone else became his master and planted in his mind the ideal of a scientific study of man.

Sidgwick was to set out, again in his Reminiscences of Archbishop Benson, the intellectual ideal to which, 'under the influence primarily of John Stuart Mill but partly of Comte seen through Mill's spectacles', he was being drawn, and which estranged him in thought, though not in affection, from Benson.

What we aimed at [he wrote] from a social point of view was a complete revision of human relations, political, moral and economic, in the light of science directed by comprehensive and impartial sympathy; and an unsparing reform of whatever, in the judgement of science, was pronounced to be not conducive to the general happiness. This social science must of course have historical knowledge as a basis; but being science, it must regard the unscientific belief, moral or political, of past ages as altogether wrong—at least in respect of the method of their attainment, and the grounds on which they were accepted. History, in short, was conceived as applying the material on which we had to work, but not the ideal which we aimed at realising; except so far as history properly understood showed that the time had come for the scientific treatment of political and moral problems.

This then was the new idea and the new ideal. 'A reverent sense of human history as a providential scheme' was ruled out; so was history except as applying grist to the scientific mill; so in effect were metaphysics and theology.

What was fixed and unalterable and accepted by us all was the necessity and duty of examining the evidence for Christianity with strict scientific impartiality; placing ourselves as far as possible outside traditional sentiments and opinions, and endeavouring to weigh the pros and cons in all theological questions as a duly instructed rational being from another planet—or let us say from China—would naturally weigh them.

Now this positivist scheme was abhorrent to Benson; and Sidgwick recalled Benson saying to him at this time that Sidgwick's generation 'seemed to be possessed by an insane desire to jump off its own shadow'. But the image, Sidgwick went on to add, 'was not adequate, for in the spiritual region he regarded the effort to get rid of the bias given by early training and unconsciously imbibed tradition as not only futile but profoundly dangerous'. In the end Benson would stand with Newman who, 'considering the faculty of reason actually and historically', said, 'I do not think I am wrong in saying that its tendency is towards simple unbelief in matters of religion.'

Here then was what came to divide the master from the pupil. This deep difference created a reserve, not indeed of affection and respect, but of communication between them on the nature of human life. Benson had, says Sidgwick, 'no inclination to argue out methodically points of fundamental disagreement where the issues were large and vital'; if he did so, it was less with comparative strangers than with intimate friends; and too great a sense of divergence from Sidgwick in deepest things created in him also a sense of the uselessness of discussion, except in the comparatively superficial things on which they agreed. This then was the issue between them; and its nature allows that Benson, though being 'unscientific' was also, as Sidgwick said, 'scrupulous in avoiding one-sidedness of view' and 'strenuous in avoiding imprecise conceptions of the data on which judgement had to be formed'.

IV

There were then, standing over Sidgwick's youth and early manhood, two figures. One was Edward Benson, affirming the authority of the supernatural and of history; the other John Stuart Mill, resolved so far as he could, in spite of blank misgivings, to show human life as strictly a part of nature, and capable of understanding itself in a way which could (it was hoped) properly be said to be scientific. Benson and Mill might be said to be the two protagonists in the theatre of Sidgwick's mind in his early days. But to Mill went the victory: and the victory was 'rapid' and 'complete'. So Sidgwick was to write, looking back from the year 1897.

But in truth, it was by no means as simple as this; and letters and other papers of Sidgwick's written in the years succeeding 1859 and much later in his life show this clearly enough. Mill himself, the new master, was not to be without reservations, alarms, surmises which did not accord with his declared intellectual aims; and this was true of the disciple also; it was all the more true of a disciple whose provenance and rearing were as far removed from the new doctrine as they were different from the provenance and rearing of the new master.

The ten years from 1859, when he was twenty-one and was elected a Fellow of Trinity, to 1869, when he resigned his Fellowship, were, Sidgwick said once, his years of 'storm and stress'. The 'storm and stress' were not in fact to cease except with his death; he was never to find peace and resolution; but no doubt these ten years were years of special difficulty.

John Stuart Mill had become his master. But, as Sidgwick soon found out, only in part. In the last year of his life he began a memoir of his intellectual life. Death made it a fragment only. But in it he says that Mill's attitude to the fundamental questions of the nature of man and his relation to God and the universe were not acceptable to him in his years as a young Fellow of Trinity; he could not be reconciled to negative and agnostic answers; and he did not, he says, break with the Christianity in which he had been brought up. Certainly there was doubt and scepticism; but these did not add up to rejection; and it was only in 1861 that he made up his mind not to take Orders. 1860 had been a year of wretched indecision about it. He feared to put fetters upon the free expression of his religious beliefs; and at those times when he was disposed to take Orders, he was afraid that he was taking up what he called 'this highest and noblest of professions as a *pis aller*'. But the balance was to tilt against Orders.

In 1861 he spoke of his need to reconcile 'his religious instinct' with his 'growing conviction that both individual and social morality ought to be placed on an inductive basis'. His 'growing conviction' of the need for a scientific knowledge of man was at odds with a Christianity he had not relinquished. Here was his problem and his distress in 1861; but the problem and the distress were to remain with him. In any case, he decided now not to take Orders.

That was in 1861. But in 1862 there was a revulsion in him, if not against his decision not to take Orders, at least against the considerations and ways of thought which counted most in his decision. Writing to his friend Dakyns in April 1862 he exclaims, 'How fearfully impulsive and unstable I am!'; and says that he was in the grip of a violent reaction from all he had been thinking the year before. In particular he was reacting against Comte whom he was now reading thoroughly, and at about the same time he told Roden Noel that he 'was haunted by a dread that it is only a wild dream, all this scientific study of Human Nature, a dream as vain and unsubstantial as Alchemy'. But this fear was only one side of the picture; on the other side is what he sets out in the same letter: 'I am sometimes startled to find to what a halt my old theological trains of thought and sentiment have come; I have never deliberately discarded them, but the scientific atmosphere seems to paralyse them.' Here Sidgwick was: between the vain dream of the scientific study of human nature and the paralysis of religious thought and sentiment which the dream, however vain, induced; and we cannot say that he was ever to escape either the vain dream of a scientific ideal or the paralysis of a life of religion.

His mind was to continue in a long interior debate which was to reach no conclusion. His resignation of his Fellowship in 1869 was certainly to mark no conclusion to it.

v

Something more of some of the features of his continu-ing and deep uncertainties and apparently incurable irresolution I shall say a little later. But here he was, a young Fellow of Trinity in his early twenties, already locked in a debate between, as he believed, two irre-concilable philosophies, the one scientific, the other religious; and Cambridge was to remain the scene of this unresolved conflict. There seemed no ground on which he could set firm foot; and already in these years there was in him a resignation to a certain sadness and defeat, a sense in him of ever 'standing for some false, impossible shore'. In the letter from which I have quoted, in which he said he was haunted by the fear that all this scientific study of human nature is a wild dream, he went on to say that he clung to the hope of a final reconcilement of spiritual needs with intel-lectual principles. Certainly he clung to this hope, and was to always; and then, in the same letter, he says that the real grief is that he seemed 'to see more clearly the hopelessness of reviving a vigorous philosophy in these time-honoured courts . . . and I, without masters, without sympathy, feel that it will be a dreary struggle'. Thus, at the age of twenty-three, he looked ahead over the years to come, without masters, in the time-honoured courts of Trinity, destined to a dreary struggle. He looked back to the days of twenty years earlier at

Oxford and the passion, vigour, and confidence of the High Church Movement then at its height. It may have been only a wild medieval dream; but there was nothing comparable now: only the clamour of many Victorian voices, all in one way or another unsure of themselves, strident or melancholy.

We are not to think of Sidgwick in these years as morose or disposed to low spirits. There is plenty of evidence to the contrary: he had, we are told, an inexhaustible fund of merriment and a frame of mind sunny and gay. But we may also perhaps discern in him a certain listlessness and passivity which indisposed him to cope adequately with his situation and to take decisions. We may put this down to temperament, and leave it at that, without recourse to dubious psycho-analytic speculations; we may say that the spirit of the age, in alliance with temperament, was enough to explain him; we may say that his brilliant intellect was gifted for criticism and the exercise of judical power of the highest order but not for the creation of hypothesis and system: that a powerful intellect did not go along with the imaginative drive and passion which animate the great systems of philosophy; finally we may say that Cambridge was the last place in which a man of Sidgwick's combined intellectual and spiritual gifts should spend his life. All this we may say, plausibly enough; and these different considerations no doubt run into each other to explain the complex state of affairs which was to produce the unending struggle and conflict of Sidgwick's mind.

Certainly there ran in Sidgwick's own mind a stream of disquiet about his remaining in Cambridge. He was well aware of the dangers of his life there. 'Pascal was right', he said in 1867: 'if one is to embrace infinite doubt . . . it ought to be upon sackcloth and ashes and in a bare cell and not amid '47 port and the silvery talk of W. G. Clark. When I go to my rooms, I feel strange, ghastly. . . .' And then again,

> I always feel it only requires an effort, a stretching of the muscles, and the tasteless luxury, the dusty culture, the noisy, inane polemics of Oxford and Cambridge are left behind for ever. But I do not make the effort from a remnant of theistic αἰδώς—a feeling that destiny has placed me among modern monkery to do in it whatever the nineteenth century, acting through me, will.

Here a sense of history, or the spirit of the age, arrested him; and this went along with his sense of a certain inertia or laziness, as he often called it, in his make-up: always he needed a master or, as he sometimes said, 'a first fiddle', to rouse and impassion him. As for his intellectual powers, he was destitute, he said, 'of Gibbonian gifts which I most want. I cannot swallow and digest, combine, build'; and 'Oh, how I sympathise with Kant!', he said, 'with his passionate yearning for synthesis and condemned by his reason to criticism . . .'.

But then, in view of all this, why not leave Cambridge and 'modern monkery'? He declined to take Orders, for good reasons. But the literary life, outside the walls of Cambridge, attracted him, the thought of speaking as a man to men, not as a teacher to pupils. During his early twenties he wrote poetry and had the plots of two novels and of a long poem in his head. But these dreams he said were crushed under the load of lectures and pupils. He said this in 1860, a year after his election

to his Fellowship. In that year he talked of going to
America, and in the following year of going to the Bar.
'I am hesitating', he said, 'about going to the Bar;
I do not think I shall go, but I may.' He did not go.
He hankered after London, out of the dreariness of
Cambridge; there was much in him which urged him
to public life and politics, in which he was as deeply
interested as he was in contemporary literature: had
he left Cambridge this would, I think, have been his
first choice. But he did not go; he was, he said, to pour
his feeble energies into a waste of sand, 'forgetting the
bright speed he had . . . a foiled circuitous wanderer'. He
was to say, a short time before he died, that the aim of
his life had been the solution, or contribution to the
solution, of the deepest problems of human life; and
there could hardly be a higher aim. But were the time-
honoured courts of Cambridge, at any rate for all the
years of his adult life, the right place to pursue it?
It may be doubted; and Sidgwick doubted it. Into
which of his many selves should he throw himself?
His friend Trevelyan in 1886 urged him to throw
himself into his social self; 'at any rate, *do* something',
he said. 'Sound advice', said Sidgwick. But 'something',
he added, 'has hamstrung me'. Denmark was a prison
to the original Hamlet; Cambridge was a prison to this
nineteenth-century Hamlet.

VI

When we look over Sidgwick's life we see, I think,
that if Sidgwick was ever to satisfy what he was to call
his hunger for orthodoxy and embrace Christianity,
or embrace it again, it would have been in the years

immediately succeeding his decision in 1861 not to take
Orders. The letters of 1862 and 1863 indeed show a
mind shifting almost from month to month. Still, in
1862 he came near to Maurice and the Broad Church,
and his heart was with history not science. A Theist or a
Positivist may have, he wrote, a very valuable faith;
but 'suppose', he went on, in a letter to Graham Dakyns,
'the most powerful informing and inspiring faith is only
obtainable from ideas which depend on a right view
of historical events—why is this inconceivable?'—a
providential scheme of human history was not after all
ruled out; and it was in this year that he wrote of all
this scientific study of human nature being a wild, vain
dream. We need not be surprised that in the following
year of 1863 he wrote sympathetically of the High
Church position and of Pusey, who had defended the
prosecution of Jowett for the heresy of his essay in
Essays and Reviews. When *Essays and Reviews* came out
in 1860, Sidgwick had written to *The Times* defending
it. But here now, in 1863, he says he is 'less and less
inclined to take his stand on the unstable footing of
Liberal Anglicanism'; and he says that though 'prac-
tically I sympathize more with the Liberal Anglicans
than their opponents, yet in my inmost heart I lean
towards the others'.

But there was no decision; and the decade of his
storm and stress drifted on; he was to settle in no fixed
belief. In this respect, he said, he thought he would
remain a boy all his life and like John Grote keep his
indecisiveness until the day of his death. This prophecy
was to prove a true one. He was not to rest in a Christian
orthodoxy though his heart, we may think, was there;
he was not, either, to rest in discipleship to Mill and

Comte. 'Take notice', he said in 1866, 'that I have finally parted from Mill and Comte.' But he did so only in part; he was never to relinquish his utilitarianism. He must be reconciled, if to anything, to some form of eclecticism, which would leave everything unresolved, and the great issues wide open.

VII

I have spoken of what Sidgwick called his hunger for orthodoxy, and no one, reading through his letters and papers or observing the impression made by him on his contemporaries, can doubt the intensity of it. We have only to read Sidgwick's essay on Matthew Arnold, published in 1867, to see that this is so. He was in no danger of being ensnared by Arnold's notion of culture, his Pharisaism and his talk of culture being destined to 'transform and govern' the idea of religion: all this intellectual snobbishness was abhorrent to him. 'Culture', said Sidgwick, 'can only propagate itself by shedding the light of its sympathy liberally; by learning to love common people, to feel common interests.' No doubt Sidgwick himself spent his life too far away from the common people, too immured in Cambridge; still, he preserved a fund of humanity which had no part in Arnold, and he would not listen to Arnold's languid patronage of religion; nor would he allow Arnold to make, as he tried to do, some sort of ally, in the cause of culture, of Newman: he saw that to dissolve religion into a haze of culture was nonsense. 'Dr. Newman knew', says Sidgwick, 'that even the existing religions, far as they fell below his ideal, were good for much more than this'; and Arnold's view of them seemed to

Newman, he said, not only 'shallow and untrue, but perilous, deathly, and soul-destroying'. Sidgwick knew well enough, better than Arnold by far, the nature of the liberalism which Newman was combating; and he well knew how deeply he himself was committed to it. Still, we see Sidgwick here ranged alongside Newman, understanding perfectly well what Newman meant, and having no truck with Arnold.

In the early letter, written in February 1862 from which I have quoted, having said that he fears that the scientific study of human nature may be only an insubstantial dream, he goes on to say that 'at such moments, if I had been brought up a Catholic, I might become a Jesuit, in order to get a definite object in life, and get it over'. As early as this, he seems to have been aware that the only orthodoxy which would satisfy him was the orthodoxy of Rome. Then, as late as 1891, in correspondence with J. R. Mozley, a nephew of Cardinal Newman, he says that if he could embrace Optimism, of which he thinks Theism easily the most acceptable form, 'I really think the haven of rest that I should seek would be the church of Rome, just because of the insistence on authority of which your uncle speaks. There seem to me only two alternatives: either my own reason or some external authority; and if the latter . . . I should not hesitate to choose the Roman Church on broad historic grounds.' Here then, starkly stated, is the great issue of Sidgwick's life. Neither Maurice nor Pusey, Broad nor High Church would do. It must be either the Church of Rome or the life of reason as he conceived it. 'I have myself taken service with reason', he says in this letter, 'and I have no intention of deserting.' But his reason forbade him to embrace theism and, therefore, the Church of Rome. 'Considering the faculty of reason actually and historically', Newman had said, 'I do not think I am wrong in saying that its tendency is towards simple unbelief in matters of religion.' Well, in Sidgwick, we may say, it led to unbelief in matters of religion; but we certainly cannot say that his unbelief was whole and simple.

We see that, after all, Sidgwick did not travel so far from Benson, his first master. Benson indeed, despite the fascination Newman and the Roman Church had had for him, accepted the Anglican compromise; but Sidgwick was to feel, down the years, the force of Benson's view and his insistence, like Newman's, on nurture, authority, and history. He and Benson became outsiders to each other; but it is also true that the sense of life he learnt from his upbringing and above all from Benson was far from dying in him. It remained something he longed for and could not possess. Therefore John Stuart Mill, with his dream of a scientific study of human nature, could not be his master either. His only master must be his own reason. He frequently complained that he had no master; but he himself made his masterless condition inevitable.

VIII

In 1869 he resigned his Fellowship of Trinity along with the Tutorship he held. He had decided he must no longer retain an appointment which required subscription to the Articles of the Church of England. He did not at all try to dress up his decision into something heroic. 'I can only lay on the altar of humanity as an offering this miserable bit of legal observance', he said.

He did not secede from membership of the Church; it was only that he thus freed himself from dogmatic obligations. But it is true that, by resigning his Fellowship and Tutorship in Classics, he took the risk of ending his life and career at Cambridge. Cambridge and the Fellowship seemed bound up with each other. In fact, they were not so. Trinity at once gave him a new appointment as Lecturer in Moral Sciences—he was not to leave Cambridge. The year before he told his sister that 'a short while will now decide whether Cambridge is likely to become . . . a place where I should care to live and die'. In effect, it was decided for him; and he became now for the first time a professional philosopher, and in Cambridge.

The die was cast now and he was uplifted by release from long uncertainty and by the thought of the work that lay before him. 'I now intend, if possible, to absorb myself in this work: be an instrument: lose my ψυχή that I may find it. It is a sublime function. . . .' He would lose his soul in philosophical work in the hope that he would find it there.

II

THE METHODS OF ETHICS

I

I SHALL now recount briefly something of the external circumstances of Sidgwick's life from 1869 onwards, and speak of his personality and bearing, and of the impression he made on the minds of his contemporaries. I shall then return to his intellectual life and progress.

Once the issue of his Fellowship was decided, and his residence at Cambridge was to continue, Sidgwick's way became clearer; and he was able now to embark on two projects of great importance in his life. The first was the foundation of Newnham, of which he was the originator and in whose development he never failed to play a leading part: by October 1875 the first college building was completed and opened. In this way he showed his concern to *do* something; and his work for women's education was not the least product of the great influence on him of John Stuart Mill. There were indeed other practical matters to which he was to give much time and great care, notably the affairs of the University during a period of rapid change. But, along with the erection of Newnham, it was the writing of his greatest and most celebrated book, *The Methods of Ethics*, which was now chiefly to occupy him, and which, like the building of Newnham, could not have come about without the influence of John Stuart Mill. *The Methods of Ethics* was published in 1874; and he was always to give time and thought to its revision for the four editions which, during his lifetime, were to follow the first. It is not my purpose here to recount his labours for Newnham and for other causes. Of *The Methods of Ethics* I shall say something at a later stage.

The Methods of Ethics was published in December 1874. In October of the following year Sidgwick was appointed College Praelector in Moral and Political Philosophy. This appointment enlarged his income and made his position in the College a permanent one. The commitment of his life to professional philosophy and teaching was now as final as anything in Sidgwick's life could be. In 1883 he was appointed to the Knightbridge Chair of Moral Philosophy. He occupied it until his death in 1900.

The publication of *The Methods of Ethics* in 1874 and his election to the Praelectorship in 1875 were followed in 1876 by his marriage to Eleanor Balfour, Arthur Balfour's eldest sister, a granddaughter of Lord Salisbury and a sister-in-law of Lord Rayleigh, who had married Evelyn Balfour in 1871.

Two things had brought Nora Balfour and Sidgwick together: concern for the higher education of women and interest in psychical research. Both these interests they shared with Arthur Balfour, who had been the first link between them. Balfour had gone to Trinity in 1866: he became a pupil and then a close friend of Sidgwick, and was among the first pupils to be examined in 1869 in the newly fashioned Moral Science Tripos with the reform of which Sidgwick had had much to do. When Sidgwick married in 1876 Arthur Balfour was well launched on his political career; and Sidgwick thus found himself the brother-in-law of two of the most conspicuous men in the life of late Victorian England. Through them he was to be in close touch with great affairs of Church and State. 'If I had any opening, any interest, I should have tried to get into public life', he had written in 1860: but it turned out that, in his withdrawn life as teacher and thinker in Cambridge, he was yet to be familiar with the play of influence and power, and the making of public policy, in the later Victorian years. No doubt he was closer to Balfour than he was to Benson; and he never ceased to be grateful for becoming a member of the remarkable Balfour family, variously distinguished in public affairs, philosophy, and the natural sciences.

II

By October 1876 the Sidgwicks had moved into the house they had built for themselves opposite Magdalene, and the frame and pattern of his life were now firmly fixed. *The Methods of Ethics* had been published in 1874 and established his position in English philosophy; he might now look forward to years of quiet work and thought.

I have said that he was to be close to the great political and ecclesiastical minds of the day; he was also to be at the centre of the intellectual life of England and a conspicuous figure in it. He was a member, from its beginning in 1869, of the Metaphysical Society, whose membership included so many representative Victorians: Balfour, Dean Church, Father Dalgairns (so near to Newman), Froude, Gladstone, R. H. Hutton, Huxley, Sir John Lubbock, Manning,

Martineau, F. D. Maurice, Morley, J. B. Mozley, Mark Pattison, Ruskin, Seeley, A. P. Stanley, FitzJames Stephen, Leslie Stephen, Tennyson, Thirlwall, W. G. Ward. The Metaphysical Society was another 'Apostles' and was animated by the same spirit. There was to be nothing comparable to it, after it ceased in 1880, until the creation, in 1896, of the Synthetic Society, of which Sidgwick became a member in 1898. The Synthetic Society had indeed a more limited scope than the Metaphysical Society. There was to be 'dry light'; but its members were incited by a desire to find a working philosophy of religious belief. Sidgwick declined to become a member in 1896 for reasons of health; but two years later he joined a circle which included Balfour, James Bryce, A. V. Diley, Gore, Haldane, von Hügel, R. H. Hutton, Oliver Lodge, Alfred Lyall, Martineau, F. W. H. Myers, Bishop Talbot, Father Tyrrell, Wilfred Ward: a company having a very different ethos from the Metaphysical Society but hardly less distinguished. In addition there was the Ad Eundem Society, formed in 1864, and composed of Oxford and Cambridge men, which met each term and in turn at Oxford and Cambridge; and the Erasmus Society, formed in Cambridge in 1872 by Westcott, Lightfoot, and Hort, but having again more the character of an Apostles society than of a theological one. Of all these societies Sidgwick was an eager and devoted member; he took the intensest pleasure in the talk they provided.

His own talk enraptured his listeners. He had an exceptional power of memory and a great range of knowledge. But he spoke always to the point, without wordiness and without playing for effect; he was never gladiatorial and was as exquisite in his power of sympathetic listening as he was unassuming and gentle in what he himself said. His book are dry analytical dissertations; his conversation exhibited all his analytical power integrated with his total personality, and encompassed by a certain lightness and lambency which never failed to delight and charm. An indefinably delicate humour pervaded all his talk. His supply of apposite stories was inexhaustible; and it was his humour, along with his clarity, knowledge, gentle deference, and sympathy which composed the enchantment he radiated. But there was wistfulness, too. E. F. Benson describes his manner in conversation: 'his gentle voice, his wise and kindly air, as he balanced arguments and statements, the gestures of his delicate hands, his lazy and contented laugh, the backward poise of his head, his up-drawn eye-brows. . . .' Yet, Benson adds, 'his expression as a rule tended to be melancholy and even wistful'. The sadness is necessary to the picture. Lowes Dickinson's account of Sidgwick, admirable as it is, in his brilliant *Modern Symposium*, does not convey so well as Benson's the soft magic of Sidgwick in his talk; but what Dickinson says helps to build up the portrait.

As he rose I could not help admiring, as I had often done before, the singular beauty of his countenance. His books, I think, do not do him justice; they are cold and academic. But there was nothing of that in the man himself; never was spirit so alert; and that alertness was reflected in his person and bearing, his erect figure, his brilliant eyes, and the tumultuous sweep of his now whitening beard.

This perhaps shows a Sidgwick in too prophetic a cast, and insufficiently easy, relaxed, and humorous. Still, the strongest impression he made on those who knew him well was by his deep earnestness and moral beauty. E. F. Benson referred to his wistfulness; and this lay nearer to the central quality to which I now refer. It was not only that, as George Eliot said, he was 'a man whose friends tacitly expected him to conform to moral standards higher than they themselves cared to maintain'. When in 1900 Sidgwick was fatally sick, Baron von Hügel wrote to him and spoke amongst other things in his letter of Sidgwick's 'spirit of beautiful disinterestedness, candour and courage, and chivalrous courtesy', Sidgwick replied saying,

I feel indeed that your praise is quite beyond my deserts; but at any rate you characterise my ideal; and it is a deep satisfaction to anyone who has to look back upon his life's work as something nearly finished to think that the incompleteness of his work and the imperfection of his manner of performing it have not altogether obscured his ideal from the recognition of his fellow-men.

These words show Sidgwick's heart and quality. Bishop Gore, taking leave of him in his last days, could only think of that quality as purity of heart.

There is abundant testimony to his quality and influence as a teacher. He had no special relish for formal teaching. But at least his classes were not large. He never played for effect; he was promoting no gospel; and he showed the greatest sympathy and kindness in getting his pupils to talk and think. W. R. Sorley (who was to succeed Sidgwick in the Knightbridge Chair) said that 'his temperament was too critical, his intellect too evenly balanced, to admit of his teaching a dogmatic system. . . . What he taught was much more a method, an attitude of mind. . . . Upon those who could receive it, his teaching had a finer effect than enthusiasm for any set of beliefs; it communicated an enthusiasm for truth itself.' He was, said F. W. Maitland, 'a master who, however forbearing he might be towards others, always exacted from himself the utmost truthfulness of which thought and word are capable'; and Maitland added that 'no more truthful man than Sidgwick ever lived'.

F. W. H. Myers, who was a pupil of Sidgwick's in the early sixties and was to become one of his closest friends, spoke of Arthur Balfour, Edward Gurney, and himself as falling into an attitude towards Sidgwick as of companions to Socrates, 'feeling', he said, 'an essential stimulus to self-development in his intellectual search, his analysing *elenchus*; and feeling also in the steadfastness of his inward aspiration a prophylactic, as each man might need it, against dilettantism, or self-indulgence, or despair'.

But with all this there went, as I have said, a complete unpretentiousness and unfailing humour. In the sixties he lectured to pass-men; and he liked to tell the story of one of them writing to thank him for his lectures and saying that they were 'the best lectures I ever attended, except perhaps the lectures of Professor Kingsley; but then his were intended to improve the mind'. This was a typical Sidgwick story. A gentle, sunshiny laughter pervaded, like his wistfulness, his passionate intellectual life.

III

I return now to take up again my narrative of Sidgwick's intellectual life. In 1869 he had resigned his Fellowship and embarked on his career as a professional philosopher. The prospect had elated him, and he would now, he said, lose his soul in his work in order that he might find it there. In this high purpose he set about the composition of *The Methods of Ethics* which was to be published in 1874.

But his resignation of his Fellowship was an affirmation, or a reaffirmation, of the 'scientific' ideal and method in philosophy. It was not only that he was now freed in a formal way from any religious commitment; it was more than that: he had rejected, if only for the purpose of the work to which he now set his hand, what Benson and Newman in their different ways stood for: nurture, history, authority. He would conduct his study of morality in, as he said, 'a purely scientific temper'; he would have Mill and Comte, in the greatest measure possible, for his masters, and write 'in the light of science directed by comprehensive and impartial sympathy'; he would be animated (at least to the best of his belief and judgement) by no theological or metaphysical presupposition, tacit or declared. Therefore, we pass now from his years of storm and stress in the sixties as they are set out in the *Memoir* and as I have briefly recounted them, to the impersonality and the resolute freedom from any commitment of *The Methods of Ethics*. 'His books', said Lowes Dickinson, 'do *not* do him justice; they are cold and academic.' So they are; in order to find himself he now emptied himself so far as he could out of his writings. Therefore, however much we may admire *The Methods of Ethics* as a treatise in moral philosophy, it does not not touch us closely, does not mean half so much to us, as the letters written in his years of storm and stress. In those years he would flee from the port and the silvery talk of W. G. Clark and get back to his room 'feeling strange, ghastly', as he said. If he was to find himself anywhere, it was not in the Senior Common Room: if he was to face universal doubt, it were better done, he said, in sackcloth and ashes. But now, in *The Methods of Ethics*, we see a Sidgwick who is a pale, abstractive intelligence, dedicated indeed to universal doubt, and vaguely hoping he would emerge from it, having freed himself.

Sidgwick had thought first of composing it 'in the form of essays'. This intention he did not carry out; the book is a treatise. In the essays Sidgwick had written in the sixties for the *Westminster* and *Macmillan's*, on Seeley's *Ecce Homo*, on Matthew Arnold, on Arthur Hugh Clough, he had written as a man speaking to men, rebuking Seeley and Arnold, entering passionately into Clough's poetry; he had something to say about all these and what he said he said with vigour, urbanity, and a sustained sense of the form of the essay required by the great Victorian reviews. It was not without good reason that he earlier and later envisaged for himself a literary career in London. But *The Methods of Ethics* is very different. Professor Broad has said that *The Methods of Ethics* seems to him 'on the whole the best treatise on moral theory that has ever been written'. This is a large claim, and one may agree or disagree with it. But Professor Broad goes on to say that Sidgwick 'has grave defects as a writer'; his style is heavy and involved, and he seldom allowed that strong sense of humour, which is said to have made him a delightful conversationalist, to relieve the uniform dull dignity of his writing. But it is not only this. 'He incessantly refines, qualifies, raises objections, answers

them and then finds further objections to the answers . . .
the reader is apt to become impatient; to lose the thread
of the argument; and to rise from his desk finding that
he has read a great deal with constant admiration and
now remembers little or nothing.'

All this is undoubtedly true, and it was not only his
sense of humour Sidgwick shut out from his book.
Still, it is also true that we read with constant admiration: everywhere there is high analytical power, candour, and fairness, a resolution to let no consideration
in the least relevant pass by and no half-preconception
or prejudice baulk the free play of the mind. 'Can it
be', wrote Keats in one of his letters, 'that the greatest
philosopher ever arrived at his goal without putting
aside numerous objections?' To which the answer is,
No, certainly not. But of Sidgwick we can say that he
strove, with conspicuous success, to put aside no ob-
jection; and it was this, no doubt, which gave to his
writing in *The Methods of Ethics* the qualities which
Professor Broad speaks of. But then, we may also say that
Sidgwick reached no goal; we shall see that, in the end
as at the beginning, he was faced, and realized that he
was faced, by a threat of universal scepticism he was
helpless to allay.

Two years after the publication of *The Methods of
Ethics* there appeared, in 1876, the first of F. H. Bradley's
great works, *Ethical Studies*. Now *Ethical Studies* was
indeed written in the form of essays; the manner of a
treatise was alien to it; and it had style of great distinction, not as a vesture or adornment to its thought
but as the very form and manner of it. But then, there
was everywhere in the essays, which composed the book,
as Bradley well knew, an implicit metaphysic; they

were written in sight, or in half-sight, of a metaphysical goal; the questions he asked drew him, he said, beyond his depth as a moral philosopher; and *Appearance and Reality* was to follow in 1893. Writing to Bertrand Russell in January 1914, Bradley said that he 'must believe that there never after all will be a philosopher who did not reach his truth . . . except by some partiality and one-sidedness—and that, far from mattering, this is the right and only way'. He says again that his own work illustrates 'partiality', and adds: 'I am afraid that I always write too confidently—perhaps because otherwise I would not write at all.' Bradley is only affirming what Keats surmised. But his confidence gave him his style; it was diffidence or, better, the utmost impartiality which denied style in *The Methods of Ethics* to Sidgwick, who was not animated, from the beginning, by the light of a goal not to be relinquished. Certainly, as I have said, Sidgwick reached no goal. In philosophy as in the arts the goal is somehow present at the beginning of the journey of creation; if it is not, it never comes into view.

IV

It is not necessary for my present purpose to recount and review the argumentation (I can hardly say 'argument') of *The Methods of Ethics*, or again the preceding history of hedonism which led on to Sidgwick's book. John Stuart Mill's famous essay, *Utilitarianism*, had appeared only eleven years before *The Methods of Ethics*. It had sought to give a wholly naturalistic account of moral experience and to see ethics as part of a rigorous 'science' of human nature:

his utilitarian hedonism resulted directly from this aim
and basis. But Mill's candour overcame his hedonism;
or at least it so laced it with contradiction that
what was offered as a system appeared only as the
ruins of it. He could not, or would not, break right out
from the doctrines in which his father had reared him;
he could only modify them and make nonsense of
them.

And Sidgwick, in *The Methods of Ethics* and throughout his life, did not break with hedonism either. John
Stuart Mill remained his father's son and disciple;
Sidgwick remained John Stuart Mill's disciple. He
might say in 1866 that he had finally parted from Mill
and Comte; but in truth he had not, and never would
do: he could not wholly give up his hope, derived from
John Stuart Mill, of placing both individual and social
morality on an inductive basis. Besides, he learnt from
Mill's mistakes, and declined to repeat Mill's major
contradiction in admitting qualitative differences
between pleasures. He was resolved to think of pleasure
in terms of quantity alone, would not decline Bentham's
celebrated observation that 'quantity of pleasure
being equal, push-pin is as good as poetry', and
affirmed that the traditional values of life, virtue and
the virtues, knowledge and truth, the enjoyment of
what is beautiful, are good because, and only because,
they are productive of pleasure.

We are entitled to marvel at Sidgwick's dogged
adherence to the hedonistic tradition in ethical thought.
For one thing, it seems strangely at odds with the
portrait of Sidgwick I have drawn, the person he was
and the values embodied in his life and thought. For a
second thing, it seems strange that Sidgwick could hold

to it in the face of F. H. Bradley's criticism: Bradley trained on Sidgwick's book in a footnote to an essay in *Ethical Studies* a brilliant burst of machine-gun fire; and then, in a brochure he put out in 1877 on the subject of *The Methods of Ethics* he brought up his full armoury and blew Sidgwick's position, as I venture to think, to pieces. Certainly, Bradley was firing from, in effect, a metaphysical position; and with metaphysics Sidgwick's scientific temper would have nothing to do. But then, some two years after Sidgwick's death, one of his most illustrious pupils, on whose mind and work Sidgwick clearly exercised a decisive shaping power and who certainly undertook to come to ethical reflection, like Sidgwick himself, in total detachment from metaphysical doctrine and presuppositions, turned in *Principia Ethica* upon Sidgwick's hedonism, and was at least as destructive of it as Bradley had been.

But in truth, if we are at all to explain Sidgwick's stubborn adherence to hedonism, we must turn to history. Arthur Balfour, an admiring pupil of Sidgwick's and afterwards his life-long friend, speaks of this in his *Autobiography*. Balfour's own speculations were from the beginning set on different lines from Sidgwick's; he too read deeply in Mill; but he believed he saw clearly the failure of Mill, out of his positivism, to deal with the problem of knowledge; and he was not therefore disposed to listen sympathetically to him as a moral philosopher. Why then did his beloved teacher persist in ways of thinking with which Balfour could feel no patience, not to say sympathy? Balfour suggests two reasons: the first, Sidgwick's excessive preoccupation, to the exclusion of other branches of philosophy, with ethics; the second, which we may judge the more important, that Sidgwick had suffered so deeply the impact of Mill's influence, then at its apogee, in his early Cambridge years that he was helpless ever to be emancipated from it. Balfour, ten years younger than Sidgwick, never succumbed to Mill's then declining power. Thus, we may think, does time and its passage play a part in the fashioning of philosophies; and it was his study of Mill and his *Utilitarianism* and not his study of Plato and the *Philebus* which we see most strongly at work in Sidgwick's thought.

V

Pleasure, or happiness alone then, is good in itself and the proper end of conduct. But, along with his hedonism, Sidgwick pronounced a doctrine of the practical reason which had never before been allied with it. He had read deeply in Bishop Butler and in Kant as well as in Mill, and under their influence he broke with the empiricism of the hedonists. Pleasure is indeed, in spite of Butler and Kant, the true end of human life and was declared by reason, he thought, to be so. But he added that the affirmation of an absolute end, whether pleasure or anything else, requires the action of the reason; and the concepts of duty, right, and good are *a priori* and inexplicable without it: the judgements which employ them, in any set of circumstances, claim a universal validity; and the moral life cannot proceed except from a basis of certain universal ethical judgements. 'I undoubtedly seem to perceive,' he wrote, 'as clearly as I see any axioms in Arithmetic or Geometry, that it is "right" and "reasonable" for me to treat others as I should think that I myself ought to be treated in similar conditions': and in respect of self-interest, justice, and benevolence, the practical reason seemed to him to prescribe other irrefragable axioms. He was well aware that the self-evident axioms of the moral reason leave us, in the rough and tumble of life, all too frequently uncertain of our way; but we must at least act, as it were, within their compass; and where they leave us perplexed about our duty in any circumstances, they may be, and reason requires that they ought to be, aided by a calculation (so far at least as one can be made) of the pleasurable consequences of our action.

In this way Sidgwick contrives, within the framework of his hedonism, to affirm the conscience as a central rational power in the economy of the mind, and declares that the categories of duty and right are not to be explained, or explained away, any more than mathematics, by psychological or sociological science. And, if we look away from obedience to the inner, felt peremptoriness of the practical reason with its imperatives to the consequences, in terms of happiness, of the actions it requires, we shall discover a widespread compatibility and agreement between the two, between reason and utility, duty and pleasure: thus does Sidgwick bring together rational and utilitarian ethics. 'The common antithesis', he says, 'between Intuitionism and Utilitarianism must be entirely discarded; since such abstract moral principles as we can admit to be really self-evident are not only not incompatible with a Utilitarian system, but even seem to be required to furnish a rational basis for such a system.' A utilitarian 'science' of behaviour with its show of cause, effect, quantities, and measurements has been reaffirmed with

the aid of *a priori* concepts, and has become, in Sidgwick's hands, more catholic, respectable, and traditional
than it had ever been before.

All this may seem very satisfactory; and certainly
Sidgwick's rehabilitation of utilitarianism was an event
of great importance in ethical thought. And yet in spite
of this there were difficulties ahead, and the ship of
Sidgwick's thought was after all to founder; and it
was to founder precisely because of the role he had
ascribed to the play of reason in the moral life.

VI

The difficulty with which, in the end, he was confronted
was this. In the scheme of Sidgwick's rationalistic
hedonism, reason appears to require of us, with mathematical certainty, that we should sacrifice our own
happiness if thereby we may increase universal happiness, conceived as the sum of individual happiness in
the world: and man should be prepared to sacrifice
his happiness, even his life, and the happiness and life
of a group (say, his family) with which he is peculiarly
identified, for a supposed increase in universal happiness. But in truth, should he? Reason, in a scheme of
rationalistic and, as we may say, quantitative hedonism,
appears clearly to say that he ought. But common
sense and the traditional wisdom of mankind will not
say so. A man, whether or not a hedonist, may hold
that his self-interest (which need by no means exclude
a due regard for others or amount to mere selfishness)
is paramount; he may add that the pursuit of a considered self-interest is the rule which should be universally applied by mankind, and very possibly to its

great advantage. If he does so, his belief cannot be shown to be irrational, and he will not affront reason by declining to sacrifice his happiness and that of his family in the interest of a thousand people he has never seen and never will see. Besides, he will have the massive support of the great Bishop Butler whom the English genius and the good sense of the eighteenth century combined to make into an eminently reasonable moralist. There can be no mistake 'more terrible', said Butler, than 'to imagine the whole of virtue to consist in singly aiming . . . at promoting the Happiness of Mankind in the present State', and he had, in passing, some things to say about the motives of people quick to imagine Virtue in this way. There is here a resistance, and a reasonable one, to a doctrinaire utilitarianism which must assert that everyone must be ready to sacrifice his happiness to that of everybody else. It is easy enough to talk about, and to seek, the happiness of mankind at large, to neglect in its name one's station and its duties, and to create in its name untold misery.

Sidgwick was therefore left with a contradiction he could not resolve. Reason in the form of Utilitarian Duty, acting out of regard for universal happiness, makes demands which reason, affirming the legitimacy and wisdom of enlightened self-interest, must decline. The reasonable law of the greatest happiness of the greatest number is one thing; the reasonable requirement of the happiness of the individual who conforms to it is another; and we cannot say, on empirical grounds, that there is any inseparable connection between the two. To affirm that the performance of social duty is pleasurable for others but not necessarily for the doer makes nonsense of the practical reason; it becomes divided against itself. We had thought we dwelt securely in the House of Reason; but now the House has fallen about our ears.

Sidgwick accordingly concluded the final edition of his book by saying that 'the Cosmos of Duty is thus really reduced to a chaos: and the prolonged effort of the human intellect to frame a perfect ideal of rational conduct is seen to have been foredoomed to inevitable failure'. A science of ethics had proved impossible, and human experience in morality shown to be not susceptible to scientific treatment: there was no intrinsic reasonableness in conduct. He did not mitigate his stark conclusion; and he had little less than scorn for Kant's doctrine of the Postulates of the Practical Reason. 'I cannot fall back', he wrote (still in his first edition), 'on a moral necessity to regard all my duties *as if they were* commandments of God, although not entitled to hold speculatively that any such Supreme Being exists "as real" '; he could not, he says, come to this position 'except as a momentary halfwilful irrationality, committed in an access of philosophic despair'. He would not simulate a comfortableness he could not feel.

VII

But in truth the elaborate argumentation of *The Methods of Ethics* was not necessary in order to arrive at this conclusion. It is plain enough to the philosopher and to the man in the street that happiness is a proper and reasonable end for all to seek; it is plain enough too that virtue, which reason also requires us to seek, is no guarantee of happiness: experience belies this conclusion. Unless we can believe in a supernatural order which finally unites them, we must bear the burden of this dichotomy with what courage we can muster: and acknowledge that Shakespeare's greatest tragic creation—the greatest of all tragic creations—in *King Lear* truly exhibits our human condition.

Still, I do not think that in *King Lear* Shakespeare shuts out from our minds a transcendental hope. This hope certainly is not expressed; we only cannot say that it is not there, somehow present in the very anguish it creates. At the conclusion of *The Methods of Ethics* Sidgwick fairly confronts his dismay. But he could not, or would not, rest in it and abandon hope. Late in his life, in 1895, he wrote to Hallam Tennyson, then writing his Memoir of his father: Sidgwick wrote at length about Tennyson and said what he had meant to him. His own mind, he said, was more sceptical than Tennyson's; but, he goes on, had Tennyson confidently asserted the validity of religious intuition and faith against what he calls the 'lessons of science' and 'its atheistical tendencies' he would have been far less impressive than he was; and he quotes from *In Memoriam* the famous lines:

> If e'er when faith had fall'n asleep,
> I heard a voice 'believe no more'
> And heard an ever-breaking shore
> That tumbled in the Godless deep;
>
> A warmth within the breast would melt
> The freezing reason's colder part,
> And like a man in wrath the heart
> Stood up and answer'd 'I have felt.'

But then, says Sidgwick, if Tennyson had stopped there, we should only have shaken our heads and said:

Feeling is not knowing. It is the duty of a rational being
to follow truth wherever it leads. But Tennyson, he
said, realized this; and this is why we went on, seeing
life in the image of a child:

> No, like a child in doubt and fear:
>> But that blind clamour made me wise;
>> Then was I as a child that cries,
> But, crying, knows his father near;

> And what I am beheld again
>> What is, and no man understands;
>> And out of darkness came the hands
> That reach thro' nature, moulding men.

These lines, said Sidgwick, 'I can never read without
tears. I feel in them the indestructible and inalienable
minimum of faith which humanity cannot give up
because it is necessary for life; and which I know that
I, at least so far as the man in me is deeper than the
methodical thinker, cannot give up.' Does then, after
all, we ask, what Sidgwick calls 'feeling' or 'faith' usurp
the place of what he calls 'reason'? Are we not back
where we were in the first quotation from Tennyson?

But, Sidgwick goes on: 'If the possibility of a "God-
less world" is excluded, the faith then restored is, for
the poet, unquestionably a form of Christian faith':
there seems to him then no reason for doubting that the

> 'sinless years
> That breathed beneath the Syrian blue'

and the marvel of the life continued after bodily death,
were a manifestation of the 'immortal love' which by
faith we embrace as the essence of the Divine nature.
'For the poet', Sidgwick says; but for Sidgwick himself

too, as the other quotations I have given from his letters show. What, then, was it to be—reason on one side or faith and feeling on the other? the methodical thinker or the deeper man in him? Or might not, after all, the two be reconciled? There is no clear or simple answer; he would not be 'profane with yes or no'.

Still, he was to make changes in the last pages of *The Methods of Ethics*. In the later editions he does not mention Kant's postulates of the practical reason in order to put them aside; and he related those passages I have quoted in order to provide a doctrine which gives ground for hope, if not for faith.

If [he says now] we find that in our supposed knowledge of the world of nature propositions are commonly taken to be universally true, which yet seem to rest on no other grounds than that we have a strong disposition to accept them and that they are indispensable to the systematic coherence of our beliefs, —it will be more difficult to reject a similarly supported assumption in ethics, without opening the door to universal scepticism.

Thus, if science requires to postulate the indemonstrable uniformity of nature, ethics may postulate the indemonstrable existence of a beneficent supernatural order; each in its different way finds rational ground and order in affirming what may not be proved. Sidgwick indeed does not make his affirmation *simpliciter*; he only says that it is difficult not to do so if we are to avoid universal scepticism: he makes no final commitment of himself.

I do not now stop to ask, as Dr. Broad does in his essay on Sidgwick, whether Sidgwick may rightly see the solution (or the possibility of a solution) of the dilemma of ethics in this way. My concern is only to exhibit the unceasing shift, sway, and uncertainty of his sensibility in its relation to belief and faith. I have said that he does not firmly commit himself to the extent of a postulate. A postulate may, I suppose, be called at most a half-belief; and even to this his 'methodical thinking' had failed to bring him. He had left his home of nurture, history, and authority and embarked on the waters of 'reason'; but he had come at best to a very dimly descried land; and he could not be sure that it was not 'some false, impossible shore'.

Philosophy, then, left Sidgwick somewhere between Kant's postulates of the practical reason and 'universal scepticism'. But there was another hope, which might yet save the day: this was science, in the shape of Psychical Research.

I do not propose here to recount the history of Sidgwick's work in psychical research and his part in aiding and abetting the Society for Psychical Research. Dr. Broad has done so in a paper he read to the Society in 1938. Sidgwick had been interested in supranormal phenomena since the fifties; from 1865 he gave time to investigation of them, and from 1869 he was associated with his great friend F. W. H. Myers in conducting the investigations; there was Edmund Gurney too, and Arthur Balfour and Lord Rayleigh; above all, there was his wife.

It is not difficult to show how much importance Sidgwick attached to psychical research. In 1872 he wrote to Myers that he sometimes felt 'with something of a profound hope and enthusiasm that the function of the English mind with its uncompromising matter-of-factness, will be to put the final question to the universe with a solid, passionate determination to be answered, which *must* come to something'; and Myers reports him as saying once that if, where religion and philosophy had failed in establishing certainty, science were to fail also, the human race had better henceforth think about these matters—the basis of morals, the government of the universe—as little as they possibly can. Spiritualistic 'science' seemed alone able to give certainty.

But, having brought to his inquiries all his great candour and judicial power, the conclusion to which he came was a purely negative one. He came to it slowly and reluctantly; but in the second half of the eighties he came to face it, and in considerable distress of mind, as his Journal-Letter to J. A. Symonds clearly shows. In January 1886 he was disposed to give up his office as President of the Society for Psychical Research: it could run, he thought, 'without further nursing' from him; and he went on to say, 'I do not doubt that thought-transference is genuine . . . but I see no prospect of making any way in the far more interesting investigation of spiritualism.' A little later he said, in a most characteristic sentence, 'I have been facing the fact that I am drifting steadily to the conclusion—I have by no means arrived at it but am certainly drifting towards it—that we have not, and are never likely to have, empirical evidence of the existence of the soul after death.' He liked the words 'drift' and 'sway' in describing his mental changes; and the fact he was facing here was that he was drifting towards a conclusion at which, however, he had certainly not arrived.

But what, under the circumstances, with science as

well as philosophy having failed him, was he to do? Might he not, he asks, *provisionally* postulate the immortality of the soul; and then, if psychical research absolutely failed him, he might 'finally and decisively' affirm the postulate in full Kantian style. But we cannot say that he ever could, or did, bring himself to affirm even a provisional postulate, still less a final and decisive one. How could he, as he himself says, having taken service with reason and in the light of all he had said about the nature of truth?

In 1888, when he reached his fiftieth birthday, he felt that everything pointed to his going away: 'I find that now my whole nature is beginning to sway in the direction of leaving Cambridge.' He gives his reasons for this 'sway' of his mind: his wanting to travel and his need for literary independence and freedom from the academic round. But he did not go. Besides, in spite of all he had said, he was to become President of the Society for Psychical Research for another period; and he continued to inspire, conduct, and aid laborious research for years to come.

The passionate question to the universe, which, he had said, *must* come to something, came in fact to nothing; or if to nothing so definite as nothing, at least to something pretty near it.

III

SIDGWICK AND
ARTHUR HUGH CLOUGH

I

I REFERRED earlier to Sidgwick's passionate enjoyment of poetry and of his prodigious memory for it. He was to give the main energy of his mind to rigorous intellectual analysis; and here the chief quality of his exertions was more judicial than creative: he could not, he said, 'swallow and digest, combine, build'. Still, his addiction to the life of reason as he conceived it never diminished his power of response to poetry: he was no Darwin in this. But what might poetry bring him where philosophy and psychical research had failed?

Writing in 1886 in the Journal-Letter he composed for J. A. Symonds he provided a clear answer. He referred to a book of essays by his friend Roden Noel, and said:

> The fundamental difference between him and me is that he thinks the Poet has Insight into Truth, instead of merely Emotions and an Art of expressing them. I like a poet who believes in himself as a Seer, because his emotions are likely to interest me more and have a fuller and finer tone; but I cannot pretend to believe in him, except transiently for the purpose of getting the aesthetic impression. And I feel rather angry when I am asked to take a poet as a philosopher.

Now, certainly, no one will wish to take a poet as a philosopher; whatever poetry is, it is not philosophy; and we need have no dispute with Sidgwick here. For the rest, Sidgwick says that poetry has nothing to do with truth, however much it may think it has; what poetry has and offers is emotion, and emotion is not knowledge. To the life of reason then, as Sidgwick imagined it, poetry (and no doubt all the other arts) does not belong. It might bring him pleasurable excitement; it could hardly bring him aid or comfort.

There is a familiar ring about this. It gives the essence of the doctrine about poetry set out in Cambridge some forty years ago by Dr. I. A. Richards: the line from Sidgwick to Richards is clear enough and shows the grand bifurcation of the human spirit to which we are now well accustomed as our contemporary orthodoxy. And before Sidgwick there was John Stuart Mill who regarded poety as 'man's thoughts tinged by his feelings'. F. H. Bradley, in the last essay in *Ethical Studies*, had great sport with Matthew Arnold's notion of religion as 'morality touched by emotion'. In a footnote he compares with Arnold's idea of religion Mill's definition of poetry, and adds that 'the whole matter again is, *what* feelings?' Then he says, truly enough: 'anything in the way of shallow reflection on the psychological form rather than the effort to grasp the content.'

But I am more concerned now with history than with controversy; and I remark how far away we are here, in Mill and Sidgwick (to say nothing of Dr. Richards), from the notion of poetry entertained by the great Romantic writers, who were still so fresh in the minds of the Victorians—and yet, already so far away from them. From what was said about poetry by the great five, Blake, Wordsworth, Coleridge, Shelley, and Keats, I choose for quotation what Wordsworth said. 'The object of poetry', Wordsworth had written in the first years of the century inhabited also by Sidgwick, 'is truth . . . not standing upon external testimony, but carried alive into the heart with passion. . . . Poetry is the image of man and nature. . . . [It] is the breath and finer spirit of all knowledge; it is the impassioned expression which is in the countenance of all science. . . .' We are not disposed nowadays to take this seriously. But John Stuart Mill nearly took the road of Wordsworth and Coleridge. It was Wordsworth who brought him out from the dreadful depression he suffered in his twenties to which the doctrines of Bentham and his father had brought him. But then, set on his feet, he took the high empirical road; and his doing so was climacteric in the history of British philosophy, and explains what Sidgwick, so impassioned in his response to it, said about poetry.

Everybody knows the lines Matthew Arnold wrote when Wordsworth died in 1850.

> He too upon a wintry clime
> Had fallen—on this iron time
> Of doubts, disputes, distractions, fears.
> He found us when the age had bound
> Our souls in its benumbing round;
> He spoke, and loos'd our heart in tears. . . .
> Time may restore us in his course
> Goethe's sage mind and Byron's force:
> But where will Europe's latter hour
> Again find Wordsworth's healing power?

The answer is, I suppose, never again. John Stuart

Mill had been, in all strictness, healed by Wordsworth; Wordsworth's poetry indeed loosed his heart with tears and provided him, he said, with a source of inward joy and the perennial sources of happiness. But in the end Wordsworth and Coleridge would not do: they were mistaken.

When in 1895 Sidgwick wrote to Hallam Tennyson and spoke of Tennyson as the representative poet of the age, he spoke also of Wordsworth. 'Wordsworth's attitude towards Nature', he said, 'was one that . . . left Science unregarded: the Nature for which Wordsworth stirred our feelings was Nature as known by simple observation and interpreted by religious and sympathetic intuition.' But for Tennyson, he went on to say, 'the physical world is always the world known to us through physical science. . . . Had it been otherwise, had he met the atheistic tendencies of modern science with more confident defiance . . . overriding the results laboriously reached by empirical science, I think his antagonism to these tendencies would have been far less impressive.' Wordsworth was no philosopher; but we may fairly interpret him as saying (and saying truly) that science is not philosophy and has nothing to do with atheism or theism. Poetry is the impassioned expression in the countenance of all science; but the imagination of the scientist is properly governed by his abstractive and pragmatic procedures; and the poet will not fear to carry his imagination 'into the midst of the objects of science itself', or be shy of claiming an authority higher than any possible to the limited purposes of the scientist. Wordsworth's confidence was complete: he had no fear of science or for that matter of philosophy dominated by mistaken notions of the scope of scientific knowledge. It was not true, therefore, as Sidgwick said, that Wordsworth left science unregarded: he only did not hesitate to claim for poetry an authority which science could never acquire; and he looked to no external testimony.

Of the disastrous declension from the Romantic mind to the Victorian I have spoken elsewhere in connection with Matthew Arnold. But the supposed deliverances of physical science in the Victorian years caused in Sidgwick, as in Arnold and Tennyson, a failure of nerve; poetry, in response to what was conceived as science and truth could provide only feelings or emotions. Under these circumstances he looked, amongst the poets of his own time, to Tennyson, who was well aware of the 'truth' of contemporary science and who, against this 'truth', advanced what he acknowledged for 'feelings' only. So now Sidgwick looked to Arthur Hugh Clough. Here was his poet *par excellence*.

II

Clough, too, had something to say about Wordsworth. Like Arnold, he deeply venerated him. 'A certain elevation and fixity characterised Wordsworth', he wrote. 'You will not find, as in Byron, an ebullient overflowing life, refusing all existing restrictions. . . . To have attained a law, to exercise a lordship by divine right over passions and desires—this is Wordsworth's pre-eminence.' That, no doubt, too, was doubtless part of Wordsworth's healing power. Wordsworth had 'a spiritual vitality' and a fixed virtue 'around which the chaotic elements of human impulse and desire might take solid form and move in their ordered ellipses'. But later in his essay Clough was to turn back upon himself and Wordsworth. There was in Wordsworth, he went on to write, a 'false or arbitrary positiveness';

there is such a thing in morals, as well as in science, as drawing your conclusions before you have properly got your premises. It is desirable to attain a fixed point; but it is essential that the fixed point be the right one. We ought to hold fast by what is true; but because we rightfully hold fast, it does not follow that what we hold fast to is true . . . because you choose to be positive, do not therefore be sure you have the truth.

And a fixed centre neither Clough nor Sidgwick (any more than Matthew Arnold) was to find and hold fast to, whether in Wordsworth or elsewhere. There was to be, in both these minds, an endless shift, drift, sway of feeling.

If Sidgwick looked to poetry for emotion and feeling, not truth, what poetry would he find most congenial? He might, as he said, enter temporarily into the supposed vision of the poetic seer, with its accompanying emotions, for the sake of the aesthetic effect; but it was natural that he should find a special satisfaction in a poet who saw both sides of every question, was *sceptical*, or at least indisposed to commit himself, and was gifted to temper the appropriate accompanying emotions. Clough was precisely his poetic counterpart. 'What should I do without Clough?', he wrote in 1866, when he was twenty-seven years of age; 'he is the wine of life to me.' Sometimes indeed he felt that Clough was 'bad for him'—he said so, in the letter in which he reported Trevelyan telling him to *do* something: no doubt, he said, 'Browning's *Statue and the Bust* would be wholesome bitters, but I am past bitters and know that I shall never burn "upward to my point of bliss".' He could hardly bear the bracing winds of Browning's verse; and he once said that some words Walter Bagehot had written about Clough could be applied as well to himself:

He saw what it is considered cynical to see—the absurdities of many persons, the pomposities of many creeds, the splendid zeal with which missionaries rush on to teach what they do not know, the wonderful earnestness with which most incomplete solutions of the universe are thrust upon us as complete and satisfying.

Here was the identity of Clough and Sidgwick. Tennyson moved him more; but Clough's prevailing mood was, Sidgwick said,

in the strict sense of the word, *philosophic*. It consists in devotion to knowledge, abstract knowledge, absolute truth, not as a means for living happily, but as offering in its apprehension the highest kind of life. It aspires to a central point of view in which there is no distortion, a state of contemplation, in which by the 'lumen siccum of the mind' everything is seen precisely as it is.

Here at least Sidgwick does take a poet as a philosopher; Clough's poetry was strictly philosophic, his vision of things was *true*, and his *mood* one of devotion to *knowledge*. It was not, after all, that a poet should not be a philosopher; only, he must be a philosopher like Sidgwick: his poetry will then be strictly philosophic. So that poetry *could*, in spite of what he had said earlier, provide insight into truth and not merely emotions. Clearly, things were not so simple as he had supposed. Only, if poetry is to provide truth, the truth it conveys must be that you can never be sure you have the truth; the poet is permitted no positive vision. A poet may be animated, like Dante, with religious faith and indeed philosophy; but then the value of his poetry must reside in the emotions accompanying his faith and philosophy; the only faith permissible to poetry if it is justly to be called philosophic is a kind of faith in knowing nothing. Wordsworth's talk about truth being carried alive into the heart, not standing upon external testimony, and his claim that it is poetry and not science which in the end provides the true image of man and nature; Keats's talk about his certainty of the truth of imagination; Shelley's saying that reason is to the imagination as is the instrument to the agent, as the shadow to the substance; Blake's saying that the Poetic Genius is true Man and that if it were not for the Poetic Character the Philosophic and Experimental would soon stand still, unable to do other than repeat the same dull round over again: all this was nonsense. How profound a change had come over the human spirit within some fifty years! A so-called 'external testimony' had mastered —or paralysed—the imagination; and there might now be neither poetry nor philosophy which was not also mastered—and in the end paralysed—by doubt.

III

The philosopher and the poet, then, matched each other nicely. And I remark, in addition, certain obvious similarities in the lives of Clough and Sidgwick.

Both had unsettled childhoods. Both went to Rugby, Clough in 1829, Sidgwick in 1852. Thomas Arnold exercised an overpowering influence on Clough; the most powerful influence on Sidgwick in his school-days was Edward Benson, teaching in Rugby, who adored the memory of Arnold. Clough went to Oxford, crowded in with the other undergraduates to hear Newman preaching in St. Mary's, talked with W. G. Ward and felt like a bit of paper blown up the chimney by a draught. But he did not like being a bit of paper and kept away from the draught. The passage from Arnold to Newman was too much for him. He must believe nothing, they said of him at Oxford, or accept the whole church doctrine. He chose the former alternative. Sidgwick went to Cambridge in 1855, and passed from the influence of Benson to that of John Stuart Mill (who touched the mind of Clough also).

It was necessary for Clough, in 1843, to re-subscribe, in order to take his M.A., to the Thirty-Nine Articles. He did so, reluctantly. But in the following year he began to feel scruples about retaining his tutorship at Oriel. In 1848 he resigned it, along with his Fellow-ship, and took up the Headship of University Hall in University College, London. Sidgwick, we have seen, resigned his Fellowship at Trinity in 1869 and took the risk of ending his career at Cambridge. But things proved easier for him than for Clough: Trinity appointed him to a lectureship: he need not leave Cambridge.

The years of his Fellowship at Oriel, from 1842 to 1848, were on the whole happy ones for Clough, the happiest of his life. Oxford provided him with a firm and congenial framework; he had many friends and a not excessive round of teaching duties; and everyone judged his prospects to be exceptionally brilliant. He wrote the *Ambarvalia* poems in his Oxford years and the *Bothie* followed close upon his resignation: it came out of his time at Oxford. But outside the world of Oxford his life lost order and shape: it took on a certain listless-ness and irresolution. His work in London irked him; he seems to have given little creative energy to it, and apart from this, there occurred religious difficulties in relation to his new post. Already in 1851 he applied for a chair in Australia; then he talked of a chair in Aberdeen: in the end he did not apply. Then he sought a living in America and was in Boston for eight months in 1852–3. But he could not brace himself to start a school as he was urged to do; and more by the decision of others than by his own he came back in 1853 to a post in the Education Office. He had contrived to write in the years from 1848 to 1853 many of his shorter poems, *Amours de Voyage*, *Dipsychus*, the *Mystery of the Fall*, the last two unfinished. But with his appoint-ment to the Education Office his vitality steadily declined, and he wrote no more until 1861, when he composed the unfinished *Mari Magno* which certainly may not be accounted amongst his best work: he worked on it until his death in that year.

Sidgwick would certainly have left Cambridge on account of his religious scruples, had it been necessary. But apart altogether from religious scruples, we have seen how often he felt the need and impulse to get out of Cambridge, to *do* something, to seek the life of a writer, to go to the Bar or to public and political work. As it was, Cambridge gave him, in addition to time for reflection, opportunity for reforming and advancing university education: something of a life of action he found within the confines of Cambridge. The walls of Cambridge provided to him his framework of life; and we may fairly wonder whether, had he left Cambridge for London, for whatever work, his doubtful health, his liability to despondency, his limited store of nervous energy, his disposition to see both sides of every question, could have taken the strain: it might have proved, as with Clough, disastrous. Besides, what above all kept him in Cambridge was his fear lest, in a practical walk of life, his intellectual life should run into the sands of the world's demands and compromises, and the universal be lost in the circumscription of the particular. Here was Clough's *Dipsychus*.

> O let me love my love unto myself alone,
> And know my knowledge to the world unknown;
> No witness to the vision call,
> Beholding, unbeheld of all;
> And worship thee, with thee withdrawn, apart,
> Who'er, what'er thou art,
> Within the closest veil of mine own inmost heart.

Then, addressing the attendant spirit, who was no doubt a part of the poet himself:

> Better it were, thou sayest, to consent,
> Feast while we may, and live ere life be spent;
> Close up clear eyes, and call the unstable sure,
> The unlovely lovely, and the filthy pure;
> In self-belyings, self-deceivings roll
> And lose in Action, Passion, Talk, the soul.

This was a debate which continuously held the minds of Sidgwick and Clough; and it left them, in their different ways, uneasy, restless, and depressed.

In 1868, seven years after Clough died, a year of painful doubt and indecision in Sidgwick's mind, uncertain about leaving Cambridge, unable to be profane with yes and no, Gladstone, who united in himself the life of thought and the life of action as few men have done, wrote in his diary:

> I feel like a man with a burden under which he must fall if he looks to right or left. . . . This absorption, this excess . . . is the fault of political life, with its insatiable demands which do not leave the smallest stock of moral energy unexhausted and available for other purposes. . . . Swimming for his life, a man does not see much of the country through which the river winds. . . .

Here was the circumscription of the particular; and then, writing to his sister in 1872, Gladstone said: 'The welfare of my fellow creatures is more than ever at stake, but not within the walls of Parliament. The battle is to be fought in the region of thought, and the issue is belief or unbelief in the unseen world.' This battle was being fought in Cambridge, in the mind of Sidgwick. Sidgwick had chosen the better part, in Gladstone's view; but alas, the battle was hopelessly indecisive. Reluctantly, Clough had committed himself to doing something—in his dingy Education Office, and running and fetching for Florence Nightingale; and his vitality slowly seeped away.

IV

In speaking of Sidgwick in his relationship to Clough, I have naturally emphasized the strong sceptical strain in him. But I said enough at an earlier stage to make clear that his scepticism was by no means whole and simple; there was never any touch of arrogance, not even of confidence, in it; and so far from flaunting it, he was disposed (as he frequently said in his letters) to 'keep silence'. There was, too, never any coarsening of his sensibility or decline in him of humility and reverence.

T. S. Eliot said once that 'every man who thinks and lives by thought must have his own scepticism, that which stops at the question, that which ends in denial, or that which is somehow integrated into the faith which transcends it'. Sidgwick was certainly a man who lived by thought, and he was sceptical; his scepticism did not stop at the question, nor can we say that it ended in denial; but also we cannot say that it was integrated into a transcending faith. Still, there were times when it appeared to be. He sometimes found repose in the thought that 'hope, rather than certainty, is fit for us in our earthly existence'; he based this thought on moral grounds: such a hope gave room for self-sacrifice and the choice of good as good, where certainty would remove the possibility of wholly disinterested action. He did not speak of hope as a theological virtue, as a test or trial of divine love. Still, in hope as he spoke of it in relation to the moral life, he found no continuing repose; and in any case it seems a hope more conceived in his mind than deeply felt.

But we need to remember that the 'integration' Eliot spoke of is in strictness not possible to faith. Tensions must occur, varying in strength from one man to another, and within any one mind from time to time, which may not be allayed. The lives of the saints show this clearly enough. We may say of Sidgwick

that he lived his life in a continuing, deep, and tragic
tension between scepticism and faith, belief and unbelief. But we are not therefore entitled to say that his
life, thought, and work were not religious. At the very
least we can say that the hope of a transcendent
supernatural order never died in him; and with this
hope there went reverence. I quoted earlier what he
wrote to Hallam Tennyson after citing the lines in
which Tennyson saw the human spirit as a child in
doubt and fear. He felt, he said, in these lines, the
indestructible and inalienable minimum of faith which
he knew he could not give up. Here at least he speaks
of something he *knew* was true, if it was only a truth
about himself. And if we turn from the man in him
to the methodical thinker we saw, as we passed from
the conclusion of the first edition of *The Methods of
Ethics* to that of the later editions, we see the movement
in him from doubt to belief. In 1880 he wrote a long
letter to an old school-fellow who had written to him
for help and guidance; and speaking in the letter of
theism, he said that no opposed explanation of the
cosmos seemed to him even plausible and that he could
no accept life on any other terms, or construct a
rational system of his own conduct, except on a basis
of this faith.

We cannot doubt that this faith was deeper and
stronger than his scepticism. Sometimes indeed he was
disposed to defend it on the pragmatic ground that it
met human needs as nothing else could; but so far
as he held it, however tremulously and wistfully, he
was bound to consider, and ceaselessly, its relation to
historical Christianity. When he wrote in 1891 the
letter to J. R. Mozley to which I referred earlier,

he declared unequivocally that, if theism was to survive, it must be by the support it obtained from the historical basis of Christianity; and it was he who had asked why it should be inconceivable that the most powerful, informing, and inspiring faith is only obtainable from ideas which depend on a right view of historical events. He never forgot Edward Benson's remark when teaching Tacitus at Rugby: the faith which had purified the old civilized world and created a new civilization was historical through and through; and we may believe that the thought of a providential scheme of human history remained in his mind an ineluctable power.

During his last illness in the first year of the century, dying as he knew of an incurable disease, he bore himself with his customary grace, cheerfulness, simplicity, and consideration for others. He spoke with his wife of his impending death, and said that it would be more in harmony with his thought and life if he were not buried in accordance with the rites of the Church of England; and if the Church of England service were not used, he asked that there be said over his grave the words: 'Let us commend to the love of God with silent prayer the soul of a sinful man who partly tried to do his duty.' But the Church of England service was used without question.

V

The qualities in Sidgwick's character and thought which won the admiration and even reverence of his contemporaries are plain to see. But, when we have given to them every acknowledgement, it is natural, also, when we read over his books, papers, and letters to feel impatience and exasperation: we weary of the ceaselessly changing complexion of his mind, his fastidiousness, his inability to commit himself, his elusiveness. We long to get out of the heavy, debilitating air of Cambridge. In fairness, so did he. But if his longing never turned into action, we at least can escape from Cambridge and seek the bracing air of the other Cambridge of that time, call in the New England to redress the balance of the Old, and read over William James's *Will to Believe* or *The Sentiment of Rationality*. If we do so, the world becomes more real to us and the ground bene th our feet solid again: we see the world take on a firm shape of rationality, denied to a world ever dissolving, or threatening to dissolve, into the mists of universal scepticism. I know of no reason for believing that William James had Sidgwick at all in mind when he wrote *The Sentiment of Rationality*. He might have had: he once called Sidgwick 'the most incorrigibly and exasperatingly critical mind in England'. And certainly James comes to us as a saving antidote to Sidgwick![1]

But, happily, it is not a matter of simple choice between the two. No doubt, if we were required to make a choice we should, everything considered, be hard put to it to know whether our election light on Fortinbras or on Hamlet. But what *is* required of us is that we scrutinize the power in Sidgwick's mind which opposed and weakened his faith and helped to deepen and prolong to the end the tension of his mind.

[1] But James once spoke, in relation to Sidgwick's work for the Society for Psychical Research, of Sidgwick's 'extraordinary gift of inspiring confidence in diverse sorts of people. Such tenacity of interest in the result and such absolute impartiality in discussing the evidence are not once in a century found in an individual.'

'I have taken service with reason and have no intention of deserting.' This was his watchword, his resolution, and his authority. But then, everything turns on the nature of reason and on what may be expected of it; and as we read Sidgwick's papers, letters, and *The Methods of Ethics* it becomes, I think, clear to us that Sidgwick looks to what he calls reason to provide a mode of certainty, reached by demonstration, in relation to matters where certainty of that order is not to be had. Here, I think, is the heart of the matter. We may say that he entertained a faith in the power of reason to deliver demonstrated truth about the universe, to 'solve' the 'problem' presented by it. But this faith was weakened in him as the years went by, cling to it as he might: and *this* faith, unnerved by failure, and his other and Christian faith, dimmed each other in his mind and left him in irresoluble suspense.

But it seems clear that, if we look to reason to provide demonstrable truth, we are confined by it to pure logic and mathematics: we shall find truth of this order nowhere else. As we move from the rarefied heights of pure logic and mathematics downwards into the world of all of us, we may and do find certainty still; but it is not a certainty which goes along with demonstrable or provable truth. It is not difficult to show that this is so. For I recall from my childhood events which I am quite certain really happened; but I should be helpless to prove to anyone that they did. Again, what I remember of my past is changed in delicate and fine-grained ways by the maturer valuations which my later experience brings to bear upon the events of my childhood: I see my childhood differently, and, as I am sure, more truly than I did when I was twenty

or thirty years younger than I am. There are here
what are to me undeniable perceptions the truth of
which I cannot validate by demonstration; and we all
live our lives, and at every point, by this mysterious
power of memory whereby the past is disclosed to the
present and lives in it. Our memories are fallible, we
know; but we do not doubt that they also provide to
us truth; this truth is not demonstrable; but to reject
it would be wholly unreasonable, and bring life to a
dead stop. We may fairly say of Sidgwick that, disposed
to scepticism as he was, he was not sceptical enough;
and we think of Hume, and read over again the con-
cluding pages of the *Treatise of Human Nature*.

The reasonable then happily transcends the range of
fully validated reasons; and what is true of our personal history is true of history at large. What is called
historical fact is not of the order of the demonstrable;
at every point we rely upon witness and evidence the
validity of which we cannot prove but may not in
fact doubt. I reinterpret my own private history as
recollection of it is sharpened and extended as
my experience accumulates; history reinterprets and
revalues the past of mankind in the light of newly
discovered fact and the later experience of mankind.
Seeley, in his inaugural lecture, would take history,
as it were, out of time in order to arrive at 'laws'
of history; but we do not need to reflect much to see
that to do so would be to try to remove what is affirmed
as fact out of its infinitely complicated setting in
which alone it can be said to have had its being; to
remove it from its setting is to create, and then traffic
in, abstractions which history must above all avoid.
And Sidgwick, we have seen, was sometimes attracted

to a notion of history according to which history must seek and establish just such abstractions. But to contradict this notion is not to say that the historian may not arrive, as his studies progress, at certain broad conclusions and strongly held convictions about the story he unfolds; he will discern prevailing patterns in history if he is not to see it as a wholly unintelligible collection of isolated and unrelated events. You cannot read a tale told by an idiot: an idiot tells no tales. But the historian will have his *reading* of history. Only, he will not hold that it is a demonstrable one: the huge complexity of what he treats forbids this. Similarly, the literary historian will have his reading of a masterpiece of, say, Shakespeare; but he will not claim to *prove* his reading: he can only advance evidence and consideration to exhibit its reasonableness and adequacy. But sometimes Sidgwick was too contemptuous of history seen in this way; he threw the name of antiquarianism at it; and saw it as at best an agreeable pastime, useless in the pursuit of truth: in the end it *told* us nothing.

Now the half of Sidgwick's mind which saw history in this fashion exhibited itself also in his study of conduct. He affirmed the role of reason in conduct; he sought, and believed he found, certain axioms of conduct which he judged to be intuitively certain after the manner of axioms in mathematics; and his book appears to be animated by a hope for a system of laws of conduct which would prove a certain guide for the individual and society, to obey which is certainly right and to disobey certainly wrong: he wanted guidelines which reason could judge infallible. But in truth the number of axioms he could confidently assert were

few enough; and too often these must prove to be, in
the thick tangle of life, uncertain guides to confident
direction. Then his hedonism comes to his aid, and a
calculation of pleasurable consequences to ours. But
our powers of rational calculation in these matters
are, and Sidgwick did not in candour deny it, to say
the least, uncertain and faltering: everywhere life seems
to break out from the enclosures of axiom and its ragged
edges offend the straight line of the measuring rod.
When we read *The Methods of Ethics* we are, with all
our admiration for its scrupulous analytical power,
disheartened by its remoteness from the actualities of
life; as I said, Sidgwick left so much of himself out of
his book; and for our part, we reflect that we live well,
so far as we do, by the perception of a rightness which
is nearer by far to the rightness we perceive in a work
of art than to the rightness of any abstract formula
or to the correctness of any measurement of consequences: we seek to create a pattern out of disorder,
and to exercise an intelligence nearer to the artist's
than to the mathematician's. But because reason in
conduct proceeds without syllogism and theorem, it is
none the less reasonable on that account; it is a living
reason, and creative of life.

We say then that Sidgwick, with a half of his mind
at least, did justice to neither history nor morality.
But in considering the nature and role or reason he
gave a place of special importance to science; and it is
necessary that we have particular regard to what he
says of it.[1]

*   *   *

[1] Dr. James was taken ill before he could complete this section, and
round off the work as he intended to do.